A Thousand Paths to Generosity

A Thousand Paths to
generosity

Michael Powell

MQP

Contents

Introduction 6

What is Generosity? 8

Charity 66

The Gift of Action 114

Gifts of the Heart 178

Gifts of the Spirit 226

Gifts of Simplicity 274

Speaking and Listening 338

The Rewards of Generosity 402

Introduction

Generosity is something we all believe we possess, and certainly something we appreciate in others, but what part does generosity play in our daily lives? Is it a habit or merely something we show when we are put on the spot? What forms does it take? How can we develop it? How do we know when we are truly giving or if we are making full use of our gifts?

Generosity can be difficult to pin down, since the purest examples often go unnoticed, but be sure that it works its magic wherever people come together and it lives all around us. Here within these pages we shall encounter generosity in all its different aspects. As you read this book, one thing will become apparent—that generosity allows us all to enjoy our share of the treasures that the world has to offer. Could it really be the path to a simpler and more rewarding life?

What is Generosity?

Generosity is self-existing openness, complete openness. You are no longer subject to cultivating your own scheme or project. And the best way to open yourself up is to make friends with yourself and with others.

Chogyam Trungpa

Generosity walks hand in hand with vulnerability; it can make you feel quite exposed, if you're doing it right.

The secret of generosity is admiring without desiring.

Generosity is a network of invisible threads of kindness, linking us together.

We must try to find solutions that do not involve self-regard and intemperance.

The off-shoot of cheerfulness and gratitude is generosity.

To abandon the need to become something in favor of being someone is to be generous.

It is extraordinary how extraordinary other people are if you have the generosity to expect it.

Generosity demands very little; generosity demands everything.

No one is picked out, no one is left out. Generosity is never partisan.

Try tipping the scales of life in someone else's favor.

Generosity blunts the sting of unkindness in others.

Life is an adventure in giving.

Resolve never to give up on anybody.

Everywhere there is something incredible waiting to be shared.

Generosity is a spontaneous expression of enthusiasm.

Generosity is like a treasure chest that grants wishes.

Whether people like us or not depends on how much we think of them.

Forgive people who have witnessed you making mistakes.

Seek to turn the tide when others are at their lowest ebb.

Only great souls know the grandeur there is in charity.

Jacques Bénigne Bossuet

Endeavor to share others' interests, not just your own.

Really big people are, above everything else, courteous, considerate, and generous—not just to some people in some circumstances—but to everyone all the time.

Thomas J. Watson Sr.

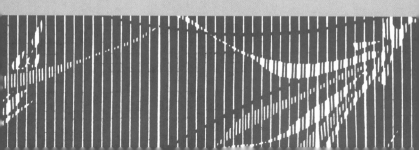

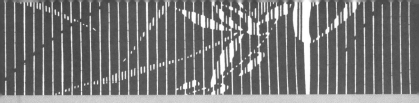

Take the feather out of your own cap to help someone else to fly.

Generosity is always asking the question, "How can I make you happy?"

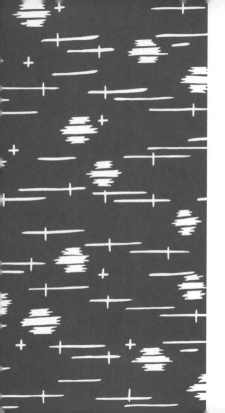

A generous
person
always
sends
someone
away
happier
than when
they
arrived.

Generosity is like looking through a wide-angle lens that allows you a view of the whole of humanity.

Lavishness lasts until the money runs out, but generosity lasts a lifetime.

Refuse to make your mind up about somebody just because they have made their mind up about you.

All growth requires a temporary surrender of ego.

Aim to put more into the world than you take out.

There's one thing that money can't buy—generosity.

There are many things that the world can do without, but generosity is not one of them.

Take a spiritual journey toward someone else's heart.

What better excuse to be better, than to better someone else with generosity?

History consists of those actions in the past that have shouted loud enough to be remembered in the future; generosity has spoken with a quieter voice but is woven into the fabric of time.

Generosity is tenderness.

There's always enough generosity to go round.

Generosity is watering someone else's garden when you could be watering your own.

Always wait your turn even when there isn't enough to go around.

Practice justice without requiring justice.

We all possess a natural will to help others but it cannot blossom without being nurtured.

I feel an earnest and humble desire, and shall till I die, to increase the stock of harmless cheerfulness.

Charles Dickens

No one is so undeserving that a generous mind cannot find something to offer to them.

The secret of generosity is when you use your extra energy to help someone else, rather than to get to the top first.

Generosity is not just something you do in your spare time.

Are you always the first to say sorry?

Allow yourself to become submerged in the ocean of your benevolence.

Be smart if you can, funny if you want to, but be generous—that is essential.

Anything that lifts another person is generous.

The most generous thing you can do for someone is not to share your riches, but to guide them towards their own.

Recognize that money is not a solution for every problem.

Generosity is
the only
thing we can
be good at
without
practicing
first.

Be the sunshine that allows virtue to grow.

Somewhere between frugality and lavishness is generosity.

Give with no strings attached.

Generosity is a beautiful garden without walls.

A world without generosity is no more imaginable than a year without its seasons.

Arise cheerfully and live the day in happy readiness to be generous.

Generosity is the real miracle out of which all other miracles grow.

Use generosity like a net of love by which you can catch hearts and souls.

How wonderful it is that nobody needs to wait a single moment before starting to improve the world.

Anne Frank

Generosity cannot live alone.

Generosity is not giving me that which I need more than you do, but it is giving me that which you need more than I do.

Kahlil Gibran

When you take something out of your mind and leave it in someone else's heart, it is called generosity.

Take the time to conceive of the best in others.

The purest expression of trust is a generous endeavor.

Give even when you stand to lose out as a result.

The generous person finds their peace and then passes it on.

It may be very generous in one person to offer what it would be ungenerous in another to accept.

Samuel Richardson

You can't fake generosity. It shows.

That's what I consider true generosity. You give your all, and yet you always feel as if it costs you nothing.

Simone de Beauvoir

**You are the sum total
of all that you give.**

Do you have
a heart that is
open all hours?

Aspire to move mountains for
others, even though afterward
they might block your view.

Make generosity a ruling
passion in your life.

**Do not wait for people to be
friendly—show them how instead.**

Be slow to take
and quick to give.

Whomever you meet, always
try to put them at their ease.

It is better to be exploited once by someone who does not merit your generosity than to play safe 99 times by offering nothing.

Generosity is always simple; if it comes with gimmicks it is also likely to come with conditions.

Generosity is leadership—
leading by example.

**Generosity often requires you
to care more about others
than some believe is wise.**

Generosity is a song that
cannot be sung alone.

**Generosity is a seed
that grows anywhere.**

The biggest lesson we have to give our children is generosity.

Always give people more than their share.

The highest manifestation of practical wisdom is a generous mind.

What we give today determines the quality of tomorrow.

Undertake to give away that which you need most yourself.

Generosity is giving more than you can, and pride is taking less than you need.

Kahlil Gibran

Real generosity toward the future lies in giving all to the present.

Albert Camus

When it costs the most, generosity is worth the most.

Generosity is the flower of justice.

Nathaniel Hawthorne

Generosity is its own motive.

Real generosity is
doing something nice
for someone who'll
never find it out.

Frank A. Clark

Recognize that generosity is a privilege not a duty.

Generosity during life is a very different thing from generosity in the hour of death; one proceeds from genuine liberality and benevolence, the other from pride or fear.

Horace Mann

As long as we're going to live in the world, we may as well try to make it better.

Did you know that generosity is the greatest tool for fixing the world?

Once formed, generosity is a habit that is very difficult to break.

Generosity is when you spend a day thinking more about others than about yourself.

Generosity involves listening to what your soul is telling you; selfishness needs you to ignore it.

Patience is generosity.

Generosity shows you how to
live your life and answers
many of its questions.

**Generosity is blowing
someone else's trumpet.**

Generosity should include a modicum of risk—giving always does.

Why should it be that we all want to receive what life has to offer, but so few of us are willing to give it?

Every gift is a message of love.

Is it possible to be generous to someone who you do not respect?

Distance is no object to generosity.

Generosity seeks to change circumstances not people.

Generosity must be built on a foundation of love, not pride, pity or guilt.

Generosity inspires generosity in the generous and complacency in the complacent.

Show a willingness to see things from another's position, even if you don't like the view.

To be worthy of receiving you must give, give, give.

Generosity means making promises while others are trying to think up excuses.

We are never as generous as we think.

Real generosity begins where nothing is expected in return.

Generosity looks for the causes of need and tries to correct them.

Be generous to your friends
and your enemies.

**To be generous is to receive
a glimpse of heaven.**

Generosity knows how to
count, but refrains.

Mason Cooley

True generosity helps you rise above any anxiety about its outcome.

Generosity is never a single act; it must be a continuum, a thousand small actions that bring about a slow transformation.

Charity

The first money to mean anything to you is the money that you give away.

Poverty is the only burden which is not lightened by being shared with others.

You cannot ignore a beggar without troubling a star.

Charity is the only sound investment you can make, because it has guaranteed returns.

Money is like ketchup;
many people have more
on their plate than they
can possibly use.

Money helps, but charity extends beyond finances.

Charity persists because so few people gave the first time.

Make all you can, and then give all you can.

Only the elimination of poverty creates true wealth.

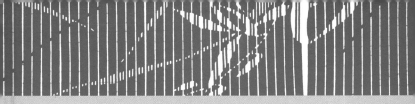

If money grew on trees the rich people would own all the step ladders.

The best thing you can do with money is give it away.

If you aren't poor enough to take charity, you are rich enough to give it.

Do you really believe that you and your money can remain together for ever?

The supreme accomplishment is to blur the line between ownership and stewardship.

Anything worth keeping is worth giving.

Would it actually kill you to give more of your income away? If your answer is no, then you must be able to afford it, you just don't want to.

As the pearls are held together by the thread, thus the virtues are held together by charity; as the pearls fall when the thread breaks, thus virtues are lost if charity diminishes.

Padre Pio

Charity isn't a luxury of the rich.

If everybody minded their own business, the gap between rich and poor would be about the same. What does that tell you? That not nearly enough people concern themselves on a daily basis with the needs of those around them.

For all the gifts you have been given, there's something else that comes in the small print—it's called responsibility.

When will we learn that the creation of wealth is often accompanied by the creation of poverty?

Don't use the impudence of a beggar as an excuse for not helping him.

To be on the safe side, give more than you can spare.

Wealth unused might as well not exist.

If you give much, people may accuse you of selfish, ulterior motives. Give much anyway.

Care less for the harvest than for how many it can feed.

We must practice charity daily. Otherwise we harden.

Giving money isn't just for rich people, you know.

You'll have more fun watching your money change other people's lives than helping yours stagnate.

There is no sadder sight than an old miser; at least a young miser has time to know better.

**Plenty of people despise money,
but few know how to give it away.**
Francois, Duc de la Rochefoucauld

Give now—do
not leave it to your
descendants.

When it comes to giving until
it hurts, many people have a
very low pain threshold.

Does your money have a use-by date on it? It should.

Feel for others by reaching into your pocket.

I shovel [money] out, and God shovels it back to me . . . but God has a bigger shovel!

LeTourneau

Just because God puts his money in your hands doesn't mean he wants you to keep it.

It doesn't take very long to give until it hurts.

Would you rather have a million friends or a million dollars?

The decent thing to do is get rid of some of your cash.

A true money manager: someone who makes it a source of good.

Once upon a time charity was a virtue, not an industry.

Never give tomorrow what
you can give today.

**You are doing less than you
ought, unless you are doing
all that you can.**

Whatever you intend to give
away—give a little bit more.

Life is too short to postpone
sharing with people.

**Little gifts are what you
give until you move on to
giving bigger gifts.**

The biggest problem in
the world is not poverty
but affluence.

The rich swell up with pride,
the poor from hunger.

Give cash
where credit
is due.

**The point is not to pay back
generosity but to pass it on.**

Work out what you will give. Do not depend on others' approval or disapproval.

Go-givers are the best go-getters.

Chase after money and you'll never have enough; share it and everyone has sufficient.

When a sparrow sips in the river, the water doesn't recede. Giving charity does not deplete wealth.

Punjabi proverb

Use your generosity to light up the dark corners of the world.

You may only want enough now, but by next year you will have redefined what enough means.

Be thrifty with your family, but generous with your guests.

Chinese proverb

Charity begins at home and generally dies from lack of outdoor exercise.

Prefer the error of giving too much to the indifference of giving too little.

When it comes to giving, some people stop at nothing.

If your idea of the ideal gift is something showy and not-too-expensive, think again.

Be thankful that you can give instead of depending on others to give to you.

Hands up who can wear two
pairs of shoes at a time.

Give now, and then give later.

Love loudly;
be generous
in silence.

**It's not how much we spend that
matters but how we spend it.**

Making money is the easy part—it's learning how to share it that's difficult.

Give now and start the receiving process.

By always taking out and never putting in, the bottom is soon reached.

Whatever you give, give the best.

Are you adding to the abundance of those who have much or providing enough for those who have too little?

There are many ways to be poor — poverty is only one of them.

Why don't I have a hundred arms to aid these poor ones calling for help?

Saint Camillus of Lellis

**The measure of a person
is what they give away.**

There is enough for all.
The earth is a generous mother;
she will provide in plentiful
abundance food for all her
children if they will but cultivate
her soil in justice and in peace.

Bourke Coekran

If you hope that your generosity will be rewarded with honor, you are not giving but merely bargaining.

Real charity doesn't care
if it's tax deductible or not.

Wish your neighbor two cows so that you may have one for yourself.

Don't just give because you can; give because you can't.

A miser's fears are fulfilled the minute he stops giving.

There must be more to life than having everything.

God loves a cheerful giver.

Where is the delight in owning something unshared? Don't bother searching—it isn't there.

Among the very rich you will never find a really generous man, even by accident.

G. K. Chesterton

Self-possession can only come through giving. In the end, whatever you cannot give will surely possess you.

Nature does not give to those who will not spend.

A bone to the dog is not charity. Charity is the bone shared with the dog, when you are just as hungry as the dog.

Jack London

Never visit someone else's house empty-handed.

Poverty is no disgrace to a man; only to those who keep him there.

Beware people who try to buy you with their generosity.

You can no more give what you haven't learned than you can come back from a place you've never been.

Only the poor know the true luxury of giving.

True wealth is not measured in money or status or power. It is measured in the legacy we leave behind for those we love and those we inspire.

Cesar E. Chavez

Giving something which you were going to throw away is not generosity, for where is the self-sacrifice?

Money flows through our lives just like water—at times plentiful, at times a trickle. I believe that each one of us is, in effect, a glass, in that we can hold only so much; after that, the water goes down the drain.

Suze Orman

Reluctant charity shames both the giver and the recipient.

Generosity is to materialism
what kryptonite is to Superman.

Lloyd Shadrach

**Money-giving is a very good
criterion ... of a person's mental
health. Generous people are rarely
mentally ill people.**

Dr Karl A. Menninger

Charity does not like arithmetic; selfishness worships it.

Mason Cooley

Giving presents is a talent; to know what a person wants, to know when and how to get it, to give it lovingly and well.

Pamela Glenconner

Anticipate charity by preventing poverty; assist the reduced fellow man, either by a considerable gift, or a sum of money, or by teaching him a trade or by putting him in the way of business so that he may earn an honest livelihood and not be forced to the dreadful alternative of holding out his hand for charity.

Maimonides

Keep money in your head,
and not in your heart.

Do not give a small thing in order to secure a greater one for yourself—that is business, not generosity.

A reputation for generosity never comes cheap.

The poor don't know that their function in life is to exercise our generosity.

Jean-Paul Sartre

If you knew what I know about the power of giving, you would not let a single meal pass without sharing it in some way.

Buddha

Giving at the right moment is often more important than how much is given.

If your first goal in life is to get rich, your second goal will be to get richer.

If the rich could hire other people to die for them, the poor could make a wonderful living.

Never lend anything when you can give it instead.

You are truly fortunate if you can give without remembering and take without forgetting.

Being lavish is not the same as being generous.

Watch lest prosperity destroy generosity.

Henry Ward Beecher

Money is like manure; it's not worth a thing unless it's spread around encouraging young things to grow.
Thornton Wilder

Can you distinguish your needs from your greeds?

Give and expect nothing in return.

Human kindness is like a defective tap—the first gush may be impressive but the stream soon dries up.

P. D. James

Sir, he throws away his money without thought and without merit. I do not call a tree generous that sheds its fruit at every breeze.

Samuel Johnson

I wonder if it isn't just cowardice instead of generosity that makes us give tips.

Will Rogers

I've never known any human being, high or humble, who ever regretted, when nearing life's end, having done kindly deeds. But I have known more than one millionaire who became haunted by the realization that they had led selfish lives.

Barry C. Forbes

Gifts are hooks.
Martial

**Gifts make their way
through stone walls.**

Be charitable and
indulge everyone
except yourself.

**Lend your support
to those who can't
repay you.**

Examples are
few of men
ruined by giving.
Christian Bovée

**A genius for charity
is the greatest of
all gifts.**

The Gift
of Action

We all have a natural instinct to give; we all have a natural instinct not to give; and we all have the freedom to choose.

If giving is silver, then persistent giving is gold.

True generosity is not stationary, but walks about from place to place.

Whoever approaches you walking, come to them running.

If you want one year of
prosperity, grow grain. If you
want ten years of prosperity,
grow trees. If you want
100 years of prosperity,
grow people.

Chinese proverb

The only way to learn about generosity is to start giving.

If you wait until you can do a great deal of good at once, you will never do anything.

Generosity is the active implementation of beliefs.

The generosity planned for tomorrow doesn't count for today.

Generosity is like a 12-speed bicycle—some of us have gears we never use.

Never suppress a generous impulse.

We are what we repeatedly do. Generosity, therefore, is not an act but a habit.

If you wish to do good to another you must do it in minute particulars.

Generosity is like a roller coaster. Once you have completed the ride, you want to do it again.

Generosity is not only something you feel. It's something you do.

Close the gap between your generous intentions and your actions.

Whenever you see someone in distress, don't pity them—relieve them of their burden.

You are born to give and not to prepare to give.

If someone takes your coat, give him your cloak as well; if he makes you go a mile with him, go with him two.

Cultivate generosity by arranging your life so that more giving will be likely.

The smallest act of kindness is worth more than the grandest intention.

Gifts only come into being at the moment when they are given.

Generosity consists of what you give beyond the second and third times.

You cannot compartmentalize generosity. Integrate it into every single area of your life.

Our generous instincts never lie to us—it's just that we for ever find new ways to disbelieve them.

When one person is generous alone, others suspect his motives; when many people are generous together the focus shifts to the need that is being addressed.

You cannot force others to be generous; the best you can expect is to set an example.

Never let the fear of changing the world get in your way.

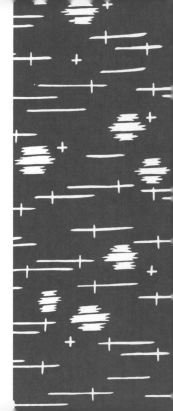

Generosity is not an occasional act—it is a permanent attitude.

We are happiest when we forget ourselves to act for others.

Feed and educate the poor and poverty will starve to death.

Generosity is the root of all good deeds; a root that grows in on itself is nothing.

You cannot perform a generous act too soon, because you never know how soon it will be too late.

The best place to find a helping hand is at the end of your own arm.

It costs nothing to remember the poor and needy; it costs more to do something to help them.

Generosity is a ladder that everyone must use to climb out of the bottomless pit of greed.

Good intentions are without any use if they are not followed by good deeds.

If you want to be generous, act generous.

Such as you are,
you are a
precious gift.

If you want to postpone giving, call a meeting.

Deeds, not stones, are the true monuments of the great.

John L. Motley

Be the change you wish to see in the world.

Some people only give what they are prepared to give. Others take themselves by surprise.

Generosity is a passionate intuition backed up with vigorous activity.

A generous idea not converted into action is merely a chemical process occurring in a few million brain cells.

Generosity is the refusal to accept the unacceptable.

Don't pay lip service; in the long run it's more expensive than a little charity.

In life try to be interested in the whole story, not just your own scenes.

Generosity doesn't change things. It changes people and they change things.

When words leave off, generosity begins.

You cannot delegate generosity.

Always give people more than they expect to get.

Give a great deal of thought to those less fortunate; it will help you to be more spontaneous whenever you meet them.

Are you a back-seat giver?

A generous act is
a generous
thought brought
out into the world.

**If you feel generous,
take it one step further—
be generous.**

The giving is the
hardest part;
what does it cost
to add a smile?
        Jean de La Bruyère

Try this: Do not commit any ungenerous actions whatsoever. Put all your energy into performing perfect generous actions.

It takes a generous and courageous person to stand their ground when walking away would give them the greater benefit.

Don't give up when you still have something to give.

Accept tough challenges and wade into them with joy and enthusiasm.

We think too much
and give too little.

**Those who say that politics
has nothing to do with
generosity do not know
what generosity means.**

To live a life, you stand a good chance of leading a generous life.

When the going gets tough the tough get giving.

Never look down on anybody unless you are helping them up.

Generosity that hasn't been tested can't be trusted.

How easy to be generous in the midst of happiness and success.

Don't wait until you feel like giving—it could be a long wait.

Remember, generosity doesn't depend on who you are or what you have; it depends solely on what you do.

Generosity is not always automatic. It takes conscious practice and awareness. Fortunately, you have plenty of opportunities to practice.

Die when I may, I want it said of me by those who knew me best, that I always plucked a thistle and planted a flower where I thought a flower would grow.

Abraham Lincoln

If we were immortal, in the end we would tire of selfishness and greed and we would want to live more generously. But being mortal doesn't prevent us from being generous now.

Words are cheaper than actions.

Things only get better over time when those with generosity of vision bring about positive change; otherwise things tend to stay the same or get worse.

The errors of generosity are better than the all consuming error of apathy.

When you reach the summit, look down and reach for someone's hand.

Always go the extra mile, especially when your feet are sore.

Don't ask if there's anything you can do. Just do it.

It's better to give something, and regret it, than to regret, and give nothing.

What gets in the way of serving others for you?

They might not need me; but they might.
I'll let my head be just in sight;
A smile as small as mine might be
Precisely their necessity.

Emily Dickinson

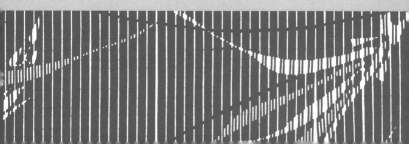

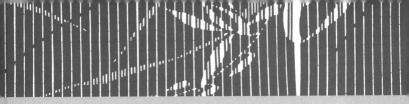

Make a conscious effort to be generous until eleven o'clock in the morning, and for the rest of the day it will be instinctive.

It is better to be criticized for what you gave than to be loved for what you withheld.

Teach this triple truth to all: A generous heart, kind speech, and a life of service and compassion are the things which renew humanity.

Buddha

Those most in need of our generosity are hidden from us because of their familiarity.

If you have yourself, then you always have something to give.

Generosity, like patience, must be consistent and continuous, otherwise it is merely occasional tolerance.

Do not wait for the opportunities to be generous; you are surrounded by them every hour of every day.

To know what is right and not do it is the worst cowardice.

Generosity is throwing someone a rope and taking the trouble to hold on to the other end.

A hen stops giving eggs when it is unhappy. Don't be like a hen—if you are unhappy it may be because you aren't giving anything.

Do what you can, with what you have, where you are.

Theodore Roosevelt

The ungenerous are not always hostile or unfriendly. They may simply be indifferent.

You can't help everyone, but everyone can help someone.

Generosity is the highest form of courage.

To be ready to give is good. To know when to give is better. But to give is best.

Did universal charity prevail, earth would be a heaven, and hell a fable.
Charles Caleb Colton

Have you watched anyone sinking today? Did you throw them a lifeline?

It's never too late to start being generous.

Always keep your feet on the ground, in case someone needs to lean on you.

Our generosity should increase in proportion to the obstacles placed before it.

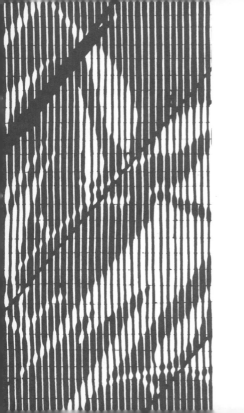

A hug
is a
perfect
way to
share
your
body.

Give me the ready hand rather than the ready tongue.

Giuseppe Garibaldi

We read on the foreheads of those who are surrounded by a foolish luxury, that fortune sells what she is thought to give.

Jean de La Fontaine

Ask yourself whether it is time you stepped aside for someone less experienced and less able.

It's easy to put yourself to good use if you always remember that you are needed.

Do good by stealth.

Ray Prince

Do all the good you can, by all the means you can, in all the ways you can, in all the places you can, at all the times you can, to all the people you can, as long as ever you can.

John Wesley

The way in which you give is more important than the gift.

Giving is the highest
expression of potency.

Erich Fromm

**Do something for somebody every
day for which you do not get paid.**

Give as you would like to receive: cheerfully, quickly, and without hesitation.

In a world filled with doubt, hatred, and apathy, giving is an expression of faith, tolerance, and participation.

You will discover that you have two hands. One is for helping yourself and the other is for helping others.

Audrey Hepburn

Give proof to others of your generosity by your actions.

What difference does it make how much you have? What you do not have amounts to much more.

Seneca

Nature takes away any inherent ability that is not used; practice charity all the time.

Nobody ever died of too much generosity.

The most important time to be generous is when you have better things to do.

Work at being generous; it is the most useful exercise.

Those who do nothing are worse than the ones who take away.

Never give too much of yourself at work—it may use up all that you have to give.

Generosity may be contagious, but don't wait to catch it from others.

If you withhold your gifts, you will suffer more as a result than the world from which you are withholding them; the world can manage without your gifts but you cannot manage without giving.

The only gift is a portion of thyself.
Ralph Waldo Emerson

Let's not leave any of our
successors anything to give.

Gifts of
the Heart

There never was any heart truly great and generous, that was not also tender and compassionate.

Robert Frost

Ask yourself this: what are you feeling in your heart while your hands are giving?

Practicing generosity makes the heart grow stronger.

The greatest force in the human body is its ability to heal itself; make sure the second greatest force in yours is the desire to heal others.

It is not the quantity of food, but the cheerfulness of the guests, which makes the feast.

One of the
sanest, surest,
and most
generous joys of
life comes from
being happy
over the good
fortune of others.

Robert A. Heinlein

The longest journey you will ever take is from your head to your heart.

Generosity means never giving up on anybody.

He who has no charity in his heart pretends to have no change in his pocket.

Spend yourself in a worthy cause.

Think the best of everyone — it saves so much trouble.

If you're not close enough to get hurt, you're not close enough to make a difference in someone's life.

Toleration is the greatest gift of the mind; it requires the same effort of the brain that it takes to balance oneself on a bicycle.

Helen Keller

You can pay back the loan of gold, but one lies for ever in debt to those who have given you their heart.

Do not neglect to help those who help you— and those who don't.

Generosity flows from a loving heart, not from a leather-bound checkbook.

A hand extended in generosity is stronger than one that is closed into a fist.

Generosity can be the first step toward cultivating a nurturing and compassionate heart.

Dig within and you can help others to dig without.

As the purse is emptied, the heart is filled.

Victor Hugo

You cannot be a hero unless you are first a hero in giving.

Generosity involves plotting to make others happy.

If you want to change the world, start with your heart and then your street.

Rich gifts wax poor when givers prove unkind.

William Shakespeare

Only the person who is generous to himself is able to be generous to others.

Reaching down to lift people up is good daily exercise for your heart.

If you feel guilty about your giving, perhaps there's a good reason.

The most generous in life are not those who give the most, but those who give the most readily.

Sometimes generosity requires us to stand in the shadows so that others can take their time in the sun.

If you were arrested for generosity, would there be enough evidence to convict you?

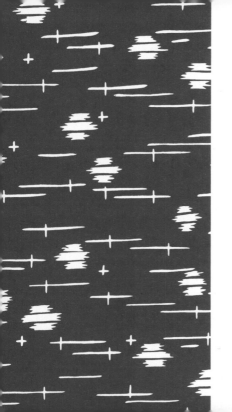

**Giving is
a game
in which
both sides
walk away
winners.**

Be happy
with what
you have
and who
you are, and
be generous
with both.

Generosity is putting all your eggs into someone else's basket.

Generosity is scratching another person's itch before attending to your own.

He who is devoid of the power to give is devoid of the power to love.

Never look at what you have left; always look at what you still have to offer.

What's the point of opening your wallet if you can't open your heart?

The most generous thing you can do for a person is to make it easier for them to accept and like themselves.

Repay an injury with a good turn.

A generous person never allows suffering to walk alone.

The best things in life aren't things.
Art Buchwald

Go as far as you can and, when you get there, go back and help anyone you didn't get a chance to help on the way.

**Generosity washes away from
the heart the dust of everyday life.**

Faith is giving even when common
sense tells you to walk on by.

**We always remember what is
due to us, but are often oblivious
of what we owe to others.**

Do not be thrifty with your love; it thrives on generosity.

Share life abundantly.

The moment that we need generosity shown to us is often the moment that we least deserve it.

We who are not unkind, why do we refuse to give? We who are not narrow-minded, why do we refuse to tolerate?

Make sure the "who"s in your life take priority over the "what"s.

Be generous to ungenerous people— they need it the most.

It is your obligation to put back into the world at least what you take out of it.

The further humankind travels from its beginnings, the more megalomania and ostentation there will be in the world.

Blessed is the guidance of one true, generous human soul by another.

**Don't live through life,
give through life.**

The greatest compassion
flows through gentle guidance.

**Some people find joy everywhere
and leave it behind when they go.**

You always, always, always
have something to offer.

Giving without being appreciated is like catching your kite in a tree; you must cut the string and move on.

If the world seems cold to you, set it alight with your generosity of spirit.

Give light and people will
find their own way.

**The best way to knock the chip
off your neighbor's shoulder is
to pat him on the back.**

Some people give wheat;
others only part with the chaff.

Unless someone like you cares, nothing is ever going to change.

Generosity does not look at the faults of others; it looks towards self-improvement.

Generosity is as necessary to our survival as food and water; without it the heart shrivels and dries out.

Generosity is a virtue of the heart, and not of the hands.

You don't have
to be strong to lift
someone's heart.

Appreciate beauty for its own sake, not for what you can do with it.

Where there is no kindness, place kindness and you will find kindness.

If you find it in your heart to care for someone else, you will have succeeded.
Maya Angelou

Generosity that does not touch and does not engage is not worth anything.

Every time we perform a generous act, a star shines brighter. How many galaxies will you have illumined when you die?

Life without generosity is a hideous death.

Generosity is what makes you smile when you're tired.

To give quickly is to give twice.

Those who cannot forgive can never be generous.

To be generous, and to have your generosity abused, and to be generous again—this is the true and joyful path.

**Instead of pointing a finger,
we should hold out our hand.**

If you gradually open your heart, little by little you will discover that we find ourselves when we practice generosity.

**Just taking a walk on the mild side
can be a big act of kindness.**

Generosity is giving someone an inch and secretly hoping that they take a mile.

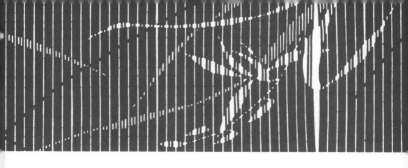

A man there was, and they called him mad; the more he gave, the more he had.

John Bunyan

**When you don't give too much,
you don't give enough.**

Everybody can be great
because anybody can serve…
You only need a heart full
of grace. A soul generated by
love. And you can be that
servant.

Martin Luther King Jr.

**The only people with whom you
should try to get even are those
who have shown you kindness
and generosity.**

When we look back, we find that when we acted with a generous heart we were truly happy.

You must give with all your heart.

Generosity means
accepting the limitations
and imperfections of others.

No gift is too small
if it is wrapped
with love.

Generosity means loving people
more than they deserve.

**Giving doesn't come from a
part of your brain; it comes
from all of your heart.**

**Give all thou canst; high heaven
  rejects the lore
Of nicely calculated less or more.**

William Wordsworth

The greatest gift we can give
one another is rapt attention to
one another's existence.

Sue Atchley Ebaugh

**Generosity is clapping and
cheering the person who got the
breaks that you narrowly missed.**

I believe that any man's life will be filled with constant and unexpected encouragement, if he makes up his mind to do his level best each day, and as nearly as possible reaching the high water mark of pure and useful living.

Booker T. Washington

Doing something for the happiness of others lifts us out of ourselves.

It is possible to give without loving, but it is impossible to love without giving.

Richard Braunstein

Scatter with a lavish hand every good thing that comes your way.

Generosity is planting an oak tree when you are 85 years old.

Consider carefully how much happiness you think you are able to give: this is how much you will receive.

If you haven't got any charity in your heart, you have the worst kind of heart trouble.

Bob Hope

If you have a generous song in your heart, it will be seen in the smile on your face.

Generosity is the daily bread of the heart.

If you neglect to open your heart to others, it suffers.

A heart full of generosity scatters joy, just as a handful of seeds can cover the mountains with green forests.

You may dismiss generosity from your heart, but God never will.

A little generosity will bring your heart to happiness, but a lot of generosity will bring happiness to your heart.

Remember that there is no happiness in having or in getting, but only in giving. Reach out. Share. Smile. Hug. Happiness is a perfume you cannot pour on others without getting a few drops on yourself.

Og Mandino

If you cannot give anything away you cannot feel anything either.

A resource meeting a need is an occasion for love.

No one has ever become
poor by giving.

Anne Frank

**Beware of enjoying the vanity of
giving more than the thing given.**

A candle loses nothing by
lighting another candle.

If someone is too tired to give you a smile, leave one of your own, because no one needs a smile as much as those who have none to give.

Rabbi Samson Raphael Hirsch

If you are generous you should forgive swiftly and completely, because you will know how quickly time passes away in unnecessary pain.

Three things in human life are important: The first is to be generous. The second is to be generous. And the third is to be generous.

The whole secret of generosity lies in learning how to use your eyes, your hands, and your heart.

You are a natural resource which you should allow others to freely mine.

Always try to be a little more generous than is necessary.

If there is bitterness in your heart, sugar in your hand won't make another's life any sweeter.

Wherever there is a human being, there is an opportunity for generosity.

When your bow is broken and your last arrow spent, then shoot with your whole heart.

Generosity is real when we make room in our heart for someone else to grow.

Gifts of
the Spirit

To know when to be generous and when firm— this is wisdom.

Edgar Watson Howe

To really give of yourself is to be on a ladder to heaven; most of us are content to stand at the bottom holding it steady for the few that have the courage to climb upwards.

A selfish person does not see the same world that a generous person sees.

Giving has a
sacred dimension.

Look at what you know and
at what you have and let your
gifts reflect what you give.

Generosity and faith are a set—you can't have one without the other.

The glass isn't half empty or half full, it's overflowing. Share the spillage!

All acts of generosity are practice for heaven.

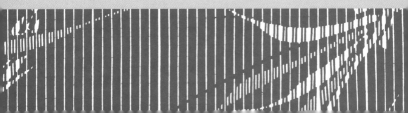

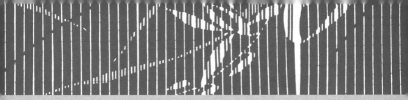

The Dead Sea is dead because it continually receives and never gives.

Generosity is inside you, and wants only to be born.

A generous spirit is stronger than anything that can happen to it.

Cultivate a cheerful willingness to let life take whatever form it will.

It's not how much you give that matters, but how little you keep.

Perform many loving acts, for they set the soul on fire and make it gentle.

The most important question is not how tolerant you are, but how you deal with intolerance in others.

The everyday generosity that takes place in private more than makes up for the acts of greed that take place in public.

Refusing to judge another is a generous act; refusing to judge yourself is the basis of all the suffering in the world.

To stop giving is to stop living.

The greatest gift you can give is a part of yourself.

Generosity is giving with the whole of your soul.

If we all gave what we are capable of giving, we would astound ourselves.

Remember to preserve a generous soul in adversity.

A generous deed means to take someone else's life briefly in your arms.

As soon as you trust yourself, you will know how to give.

Remind yourself regularly that you are more capable of tolerance than you think you are.

Always apply your mind to what the other person wants.

If you feel that others don't pay you enough regard, the reason is likely to be that you haven't contributed anything to their happiness.

Fashion your life as a garland of generous deeds.

Poverty might steal your wealth, but it can't touch your generosity.

Make generosity your religion.

If the good deeds you have performed today were fish, would you throw them back in the river?

Generosity removes the rust from the mind and allows our thoughts to shine through our actions.

When eating bamboo sprouts, remember the man who planted them.

Chinese proverb

Do not worry that what you give seems only a drop in the ocean; the ocean is made up of drops.

You are richer today if you have laughed, given, or forgiven.

Generosity is the rent we pay for living on earth.

When you wake in the morning, give thanks for the new day, for your life and strength.

No act of generosity was ever accomplished without two things: enthusiasm and humility.

If you want happiness for an hour, take a nap. If you want happiness for a day, go fishing. If you want happiness for a year, inherit a fortune. If you want happiness for a lifetime, help somebody.

A simple act of generosity is capable of wiping out the lean years and makes the spirit shine again.

You must give two things: what you have and what you are.

Generosity is a higher revelation than philosophy.

You give the thing you think you cannot give.

The generous see generosity; the wise see wisdom. You only see in the world what you give out to it.

If life is going badly, it's easy to blame it on someone else— so whom do you credit for the good times?

No act of kindness, no matter how small, is ever wasted.

Aesop

The only way to explore the limits of your generosity is by going beyond them.

If you had the choice between a generous nature and a quiet conscience, choose the first, because the second is thrown in for free.

If you're a generous person you'll have no trouble admitting that somebody else is good.

It is one thing not to know what you want, but quite another to have no one to share it with when you get it.

Make your thinking generous and objective, and you will see the world with clarity and charity.

A generous soul is the home of paradise.

As soon as you make up your mind to be a kinder and more liberal person you will discover opportunities for generosity all around you.

The art of being generous is the art of overlooking nobody.

Giving isn't always generous;
taking isn't always selfish.

Don't just give away,
give back as well.

**Talent is always conscious
of its own abundance, and
does not object to sharing.**
Aleksandr Solzhenitsyn

You are the only person on this earth
who can give what you can give.

Give freely even
if you can't give
bountifully.

**When you see ungenerous people,
reflect inwardly on yourself.**

Make your joys as deep as the ocean,
and your sorrows as light as its foam.

The essence of generosity is gratitude.

Life is short but there is always time for generosity.

The meek will inherit the earth; and they'll happily share it with the rest of us.

Some people don't like to be generous because they're afraid of setting a precedent.

Generosity is a principle— not a figure.

Although the world is full of selfishness, it is full also of the overcoming of it.

To give requires good sense.

Ovid

Do you have the right to consume happiness without producing it?

To give alms is nothing unless you give thought also. A little thought and a little kindness are often worth more than a great deal of money.

John Ruskin

The hands give poorly when the eyes are full of pride.

The greatest science in the world is generosity.

Generosity is a curious commodity; you can give 110 per cent and find you still have plenty left over.

Cultivate generosity by enlarging your imagination.

The responsibility of tolerance lies in those who have the wider vision.

George Eliot

We do not give in proportion to what we have; we give in proportion to the amount of humanity we possess.

Loyalty is a variation on generosity—
you give your trust and faith.

**Generosity is something that
everyone should try at least once in
their lifetime.**

Generosity is trust in what
the spirit already knows.

**Of all the varieties of virtue,
liberality is the most beloved.**

Aristotle

Generosity is very
good lubrication for
the soul.

**The most generous
person is the one who
doesn't think he is.**

Arrange whatever pieces come your way and share whatever picture you can make.

Being alive serves no purpose if one has nothing to give.

It is wonderful to give when you are asked, but it is preferable to give before someone asks, through an understanding of their needs.

Generosity is always wise.
Winston Churchill

Be generous, and then you may be sure that there is one less selfish person in the world.

Health and generosity mutually beget each other.

Life is like a great ship loaded with cargo to be delivered to many different people in many different places. You are the captain. God is the owner.

The surest way to be generous is to assume that you know less than everyone else.

An ungenerous man is one who never changes his mind.

Ideas must work their way through the brains and arms of men, or they are no better than dreams.

Ralph Waldo Emerson

Being generous, when you know it will cost you, is the true test of generosity.

People who think they're generous to a fault usually think that's their only fault.

Sydney J. Harris

The best way to make a dream more real is to share it.

Never do anything ungenerous, even if the law permits it.

Tell me how you treat others and I'll tell you what you are.

If you can give only one gift, let it be enthusiasm.

If you want to be generous, you must start by being generous with yourself.

You know how selfish the average person can be? Well, many of them can be even more selfish than that.

When you give, a part of you remains with the gift and the giver.

Be generous.
It is a way of being wise.

Generosity is born out of a feeling of gratitude.

Generosity is compassion carried through to its logical conclusion.

Imagine what a harmonious world it could be if every single person, both young and old shared a little of what he is good at doing.

Quincy Jones

He has the right to criticize who has the heart to help.
Abraham Lincoln

Organize your life so that you earn spiritual interest on the money you give away.

Giving is
true having.

Generosity is the oil which keeps the spirit burning.

God's gifts put ours to shame.

Give what you have.
To someone it may be better
than you dare to think.

Henry Wadsworth Longfellow

The fragrance remains in the hand that gave the rose.

Guide your spirit towards simplicity rather than accumulation.

Adapt yourself cheerfully to new things and share your good humor with others.

If you want to be liked, be generous with who you are.

Consider how appropriate are the gifts you give rather than how much they cost.

When the giving goes, everything goes.

**The cultivation of generosity
can be an opportunity for deep
self-observation and curiosity
as well as an exercise in giving.**

Always show hospitality to
strangers: unwittingly you may
be entertaining an angel.

Enthusiasm is the greatest asset to a generous soul.

All my experience of the world teaches me that in 99 cases out of 100, the safe and just side of a question is the generous and merciful side.

Anna Jameson

Follow your passion; ungenerous people are the way they are because they are compensating for the fact that they have traveled so far away from their passion that it is almost out of sight.

Don't stop giving until God stops giving to you.

Liberalism—it is well to recall this today—is the supreme form of generosity; it is the right which the majority concedes to minorities and hence it is the noblest cry that has ever resounded in this planet.

Jose Ortega y Gasset

Whatever you do for yourself dies with you. What you do for others will remain for ever.

Gifts of
Simplicity

In my hut this spring,
there is nothing—
there is everything!

Sodo

**Giving is simple, but
we insist on making it
complicated.**

Be absolutely determined to enjoy whatever you are doing. That's a gift to yourself.

Selfishness is measured by what we can carry; generosity by what we can set down.

Generosity is not giving someone a cup; generosity is pouring the contents of your cup into theirs.

There is no generosity where there is not simplicity, kindness, and truth.

What we need is more people who specialize in giving.

Everything you need you already have.

Every increased possession adds to our burden.

**It's impossible to hold two
watermelons in one hand.
Don't take more than you need.**

If you wish to be
generous, don't at the
same time wish for ten
other incompatible things.

Give many gifts—
that's what they're
there for.

**All who would win joy, must share it;
happiness was born a twin.**

Lord Byron

We pity in generalities, but we give in details.

A taste for simplicity allows tolerance and liberality to grow.

Search for ways to win that don't involve beating others.

Life is generosity.
If you miss
generosity,
you miss life.

**Kindness is
as much an
absence of
selfishness
as a surfeit
of generosity.**

A generous person lives in a generous world. A selfish person lives in a selfish world.

Give something worth remembering.

Generosity does not measure; it just gives.

People who are sensible about generosity are incapable of it.

Be more generous:
don't follow the path of
least assistance.

Forgiveness is a gift of high value. Yet its cost is nothing.

Betty Smith

Surprise people with little acts of kindness.

Give of yourself as though you were cooking a small fish—don't overdo it.

Be as indiscriminate in your giving as you are in your acquiring.

What you put in, you take away.

One person with a generous spirit, is equal to 99 who only think of themselves.

How many things are there in the world which you do not need; how many of these do you already own?

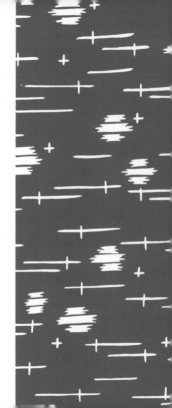

The sun will set without your assistance. Divert your attention to more deserving cases.

Give as simply as possible.

The best things that can come into your life are gifts for other people.

Have you noticed how much easier it is to scratch someone else's back than your own?

God does not ask your ability or your inability. He asks only your availability.

Mary Kay Ash

The best and most beautiful
things in the world cannot be
seen or even touched. They
must be given.

**Anything that has real and lasting
value is always a gift from within.**
Franz Kafka

Store up treasures on earth and every day that passes will take you farther away from them; store up treasures in heaven and you are constantly moving toward them.

Generosity is not a means to an end. It is both the means and the end.

Provision for others is a fundamental responsibility of human life.
Woodrow Wilson

Generosity is like a fruit in season at all times.

Every morning prepare your soul for a generous day.

Magnanimous gestures have the greatest effect when that isn't their purpose.

Surviving
adversity is
difficult, but
surviving
prosperity
is harder.

A single person performing a generous act is better than a thousand heads bowing in prayer.

Be generous—and mighty forces will come to your aid.

Sharing is sometimes more demanding than giving.

Mary Bateson

Giving breaks us out of orbit around our possessions.

Arm yourself with generosity rather than criticisms; wear humility rather than fine clothes.

Give one gift at a time and, before you know it, you've created a pile of treasures.

New gifts waiting to
be discovered will
come to us as we
use and share
what has already
been given.

Rodney Romney

If you want to be rich, give!
If you want to be poor, grasp!

Nothing can defend itself against generosity.

There is only one kind of
selfishness; there are a
thousand types of generosity.

If you take and never give, though you may last for years, you'll never really live.

Slow down, simplify, and be generous.

Send someone a gift without saying whom it is from.

Nothing is as true as what one gives.

May you live in generous times.

Hoarding is like holding your breath; generosity is like breathing out.

The gifts that one receives
for giving are so
immeasurable that it is
almost an injustice to
accept them.

Rod Mckuen

Generosity is about being yourself in every thought and deed.

Generosity provides the way out of every situation that has no way out.

Generosity is not a place to arrive at, but a way of traveling.

Selfishness is
the real sacrifice
of self.

Life is all about give and take, but mostly give.

How much a year do you spend on prestige?

If you are all wrapped up in yourself, you are overdressed.

Every charitable act is a stepping stone towards heaven.

Henry Ward Beecher

Generosity means opening your mind, even when it's empty.

Generous people make the best teachers because they share their knowledge instead of showing what they know.

Anything that is
of value in life
only multiplies
when it is given.
Deepak Chopra

Peace begins when the hungry are fed.

The habit of giving only enhances the desire to give.

Walt Whitman

If you can't be content with what you have received, be thankful for what you have escaped.

If we had to carry all our money, no one would have more than they could carry.

If life hands you a lemon, hang on to it; you never know when you'll meet someone who has never seen a lemon before.

Generosity is a circle: you can start anywhere and need never stop.

If a million
people act selfishly,
it still doesn't
make it right.

Let your generosity guide you, and then follow that guidance without fear or regret.

The human contribution is the essential ingredient. It is only in the giving of oneself to others that we truly live.

Ethel Percy Andrus

Beneficence is a duty; and he who frequently practices it and sees his benevolent intentions realized, at length comes to love him to whom he has done good.

Immanual Kant

Generously celebrate the diversity of human nature; if we were all the same, all but one of us would be surplus to requirement.

One can't be sincere and grasp at the same time.

The purpose of life is discovering the things you are good at; the meaning of life is sharing them.

Half the work that is done in the world is done in order to hang on to stuff.

He who gives first,
gives best.

**Never forget that one
great simple gift can
change everything.**

Build bridges
instead of walls.

Keep your fears to yourself, but share your courage with others.

Relax your grip on all of life's paraphernalia and give generosity a chance to breathe.

Make room for others even when you're in a tight spot.

There are no short cuts to generosity.

Generosity is impoverished by impatience.

If only our impulse to give could match our impulse to possess.

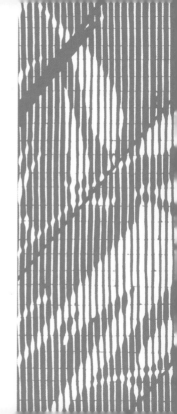

In your life, do not fall into the trap of chasing after the trappings.

While humans clog up their lives with junk, every other animal in the world is busy living.

There is nothing we can offer to others more precious than our talents.

Nothing is really over until the moment you stop giving.

Build upon generosity, and selfishness will take care of itself.

Live simply, so others may simply live.

I have found that among its other benefits, giving liberates the soul of the giver.

Maya Angelou

Three things you can't be: a little bit dead, a little bit pregnant, and a little bit generous.

Do not mistake the vanity of giving for true liberality.

Generosity is not needing to feel in charge all the time.

To know the value of generosity, it is necessary to have suffered from the cold indifference of others.

Eugene Cloutier

The mark of a generous action is that it appears essential in retrospect.

Your wealth will always enlarge rather than satisfy your appetites.

Just as there are no half-truths, there are no small gifts.

If you cannot show generosity right where you are, where else do you expect to show it?

Aim to take less even when you know you can get more than you've taken.

The most wasted day is the one during which you did not give.

It's better to be
generous than wise.

**The opposite of generosity
is apathy—or is it envy?**

Don't try to be more generous than your contemporaries. Try to be more generous than yourself.

The brief gratification of getting rarely matches the never-ending joy of giving.

Are your fellow humans
enlarged or reduced as a
result of your help? Have you
made them bigger or smaller?
More able or less able?

Neale Donald Walsch

When you see someone without a smile, give them one of yours.

To be generous is to eliminate the unnecessary so that we may all share what is necessary.

Those who wish to give always find a gift.

If you can't help a hundred people, then help just one.

Few rich men own their things. The things own them.

If you wish to travel far and fast, travel light.

The world consists of other people; everything else is a distraction.

We hold on so tightly that our hands are unavailable to reach out for the happiness we could gain by letting go.

M. J. Ryan

Speaking
and Listening

A kind word is
like a spring day.

**What do we live for,
if it is not to make life less
difficult for each other?**

George Eliot

If someone planted an acorn in front of your house for every kind word you ever spoke and chopped down a tree for every unkind word, would your garden be a forest or a desert?

There is no substitute for speaking your mind—be generous with your honesty.

Generosity is a beautiful poem without words.

Always remember there are certain people who set their watches by your clock.

The more sympathy you give, the less you need.

**The fewest words are worthwhile
if they are filled with generosity.**

Grudge-giving says, "I must."
Duty-giving says, "I should."
Thanks-giving says, "I want to."

Generosity in words creates confidence, generosity in thinking creates depth, but generosity in feeling creates love.

See if you can give yourself gifts such as self-acceptance or sitting quietly without feeling the need to say anything.

Intelligent people are comfortable about sharing their thoughts, because they know that they have plenty more in their head.

Avoid flattery; it is not a gift since it corrupts both the receiver and the giver.

It is no coincidence that when giving to someone we say, "Here," because we are truly living in the present and making full use of that moment.

The world would be a happier place if we all learned to use these four simple words: "This is for you."

All people give in the same language.

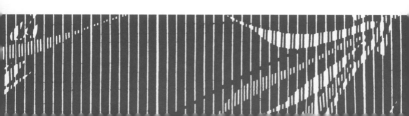

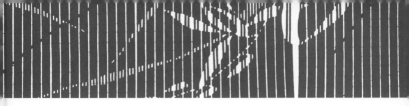

**Speak in the belief that
what you say makes a
difference. It does.**

Any excuse for
generosity is good
enough.

The
generous
person lets
others do
the talking.

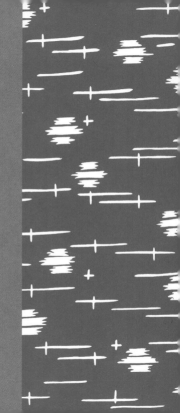

Generosity is flattering people with absolute sincerity.

Generosity is more than words; more than actions; it is a joyful expression of humanity.

Laugh at yourself often and invite others to join in.

Some people think they are generous because they give away free advice.

Elegance of language doesn't always come from the smartest people; it comes from those who can empathize with their fellows and share a common experience.

Sometimes the
most generous thing
you can say is,
"I am not yet able to
be sure about this."

You are forgiven for your happiness and your successes only if you generously consent to share them.

Albert Camus

Only generous people can learn; you have to allow new ideas and concepts to enter your consciousness with a kind of cheerful openness.

Generous words allow the genius in others to blossom.

Generosity springs from a refusal to say, "That's just the way it is."

Generosity is whatever you do after you stop talking about what you are going to do.

Give help rather than advice.

Generosity is not allowing your mouth to say anything your heart can't back up.

Give more than other people if you can, but do not tell them about it.

**When you contribute
to someone's sense of
self-worth and self-esteem,
you give them more than
money can buy.**

We move in a river of talk
when we should be bathing in
the milk of human kindness.

The whole of life is in the verb giving.

If the only thing you said in your whole life was, "Have this," that would suffice.

One of the most valuable things we can do to heal one another is listen to each other's stories.

Rebecca Falls

The most generous people are the ones who do more listening than talking.

Generosity is the ability to listen to almost anything without losing your temper or your self-belief.

The first duty
of generosity is
to listen.

**Listen to your conscience:
it will tell you how much
to give.**

We have a million reasons for putting ourselves first, but not a single excuse.

The greatest pleasure in life is giving what people say you cannot give.

A generous person speaks more kindly to his enemies than an ungenerous person does to his friends.

Whenever you hear someone ask, "Why did this happen to me?" help them see the joy that will soon come their way.

Everyone needs generosity directed toward them, especially those who say they can manage on their own.

Generous encouragement can be a high spot in someone's life; you never know when your words will transform and heal.

The true spirit of generosity consists in building on another person's words, not overturning them.

If you want to light up a room, take a shine to the people who are there.

One kind word can warm three winter months.

Japanese proverb

Be kind, for everyone you meet is fighting a hard battle.

Anything will grow if it is appreciated.

If you don't like someone,
make a point of getting to
know them better.

**Be a good listener. Your ears will
never get you in trouble.**

Frank Tyger

Givers make friends easily because of their ability to give of themselves.

People are remarkable in their generosity if someone just tells them the need is there.

Before you blame,
see first if you
can't excuse.

**Reversing your treatment of a
person you have wronged is more
generous than asking forgiveness.**

Credit people with qualities that they may not possess.

As water will wear away rock, generous words will wear away the hardest of hearts.

If you wish to lift the world forward and upward, aim to encourage more than criticize.

The best thing to lend people is your ears.

It is difficult for anyone to speak when you only listen to yourself.

Generosity
happens
when we stop
broadcasting
and start
receiving.

**Sometimes
generous words
are even better
than silence.**

Occasionally proving that you are right is a gift, but the rest of the time it's theft.

Share our similarities, rejoice in our differences.

Listen if you want to give. Don't explain or justify—that is to take.

There is
no greater
gift than a
listening
ear.

**Try to
understand
the things
that you
fear.**

A bad gift is better than a good excuse.

Translating your appreciation of someone into words is all that is necessary to make a day.

Never belittle anyone's ambitions or laugh at their dreams.

Have you had a kindness shown?
Pass it on;
Twas not given for thee alone,
Pass it on;
Let it travel down the years,
Let it wipe another's tears,
Till in Heaven the deed appears,
Pass it on.

Henry Burton

It takes less time to give than it does to think up an excuse for not giving.

An ounce of help is better than a pound of preaching.

Generous words create a world full of possibilities.

Announce your goals and disguise your achievements.

Be generous with kindly words, especially about those who are absent.

Johann Wolfgang von Goethe

Generosity transforms "us" and "them" into "we."

Whenever you get the opportunity to say a kind word, take it.

If the world is to grow toward its full potential, we must encourage each other with generosity, sincerity, and intelligence.

Beware people who appear to show you generosity but don't listen to what you have to say.

One promises much to avoid giving little.

Difficult as it is really to listen to someone in affliction, it is just as difficult for him to know that compassion is listening to him.

Simone Weil

Generosity is reminding someone else that they are special.

A generous person has the ability to listen to somebody that they have nothing in common with and still be fascinated by their presence.

Generous
words are never
interrupted.

It does not require many
words to speak the language
of generosity.

Your own words are the bricks and mortar of the world you want to build for others.

We all of us deserve happiness or none of us does.

Mary Gordon

If you can offer someone a word of encouragement during a failure it will mean more to them than an hour of praise after success.

The difference between selfishness and generosity? You need an excuse to be selfish.

No person was ever honored for what he received. Honor has been the reward for what he gave.

Calvin Coolidge

God speaks through generous hands, and smiles behind cheerful eyes.

There is more hunger for kind words in this world than for bread.

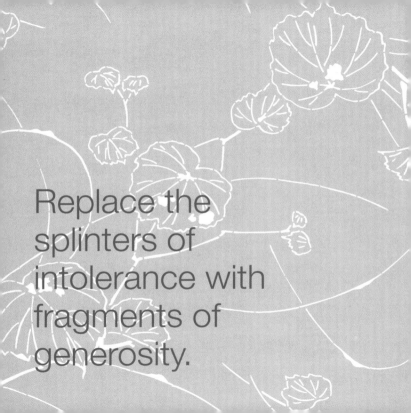

Replace the
splinters of
intolerance with
fragments of
generosity.

Generous people may be calm or impassioned in their speech, subtle or rugged, urbane or naïve, but they are always pleasant company.

Letter-writing on the part of a busy man or woman is the quintessence of generosity.

Agnes Repplier

Generosity is often the best means of persuasion.

The words which express our generosity are carried like seeds on the winds of change.

Too often we underestimate the power of a touch, a smile, a kind word, a listening ear, an honest compliment, or the smallest act of caring, all of which have the potential to turn a life around.

Leo Buscaglia

Look, listen, learn, give, lead.

The most basic of all human needs is the need to understand and be understood. The best way to understand people is to listen to them.
Ralph Nichols

Generosity is eye contact and a hand placed gently upon an arm.

Words have no meaning
without people behind them.

**Generosity means
wrapping a subtle layer
of kindness around
your words.**

Remember that everyone you
meet in this life has something
to teach you.

Listen to your head and your heart. If they disagree, follow your heart.

All language is wasted until it finds a generous and attentive listener.

Generosity is listening to someone talk about themselves when you want to talk about yourself.

You can't put yourself in someone else's shoes until you take off your own.

If you don't see eye to eye with someone, try to hear ear to ear.

Be generous by revealing to someone that they really are worth listening to.

Kind words can be short and easy to speak, but their echoes are truly endless.

Mother Theresa

Speak and act generously—selfish thoughts, words, and actions always return to confront you.

When you speak, remember that mostly people want to hear what's in your heart.

**Generosity
is like an
uninterrupted
prayer.**

When you are
generous with your
words, they
overflow beyond
family and friends—
they reach out to
everyone you meet.

Give naught,
get same.
Give much,
get same.

Malcolm Forbes

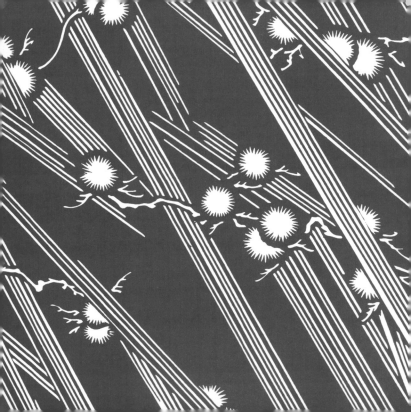

The Rewards
of Generosity

I don't know what your destiny will be, but one thing I do know: the only ones among you who will be really happy are those who have sought and found how to serve.

Albert Schweitzer

None of us move forward without each other.

Three grand essentials to happiness in this life are something to give, someone to give it to, and a ribbon.

**Support the strong, give courage
to the timid, remind the indifferent,
and warn the opposed.**

Whitney M. Young

The interconnectedness of all life
does not have to be an abstract
concept. We can live it by extending
a hand to our neighbors.

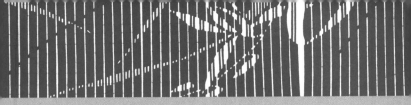

Possessions are like grains of sand; we can fill our pockets with them or share them to create a beautiful beach.

When we are generous we affect eternity; we can never tell where our influence stops.

Raise your standard of living by raising your standard of giving.

Generosity means spurring on others to give by setting an example.

It's not always apparent what you get back from a generous action, but don't get hung up on the obvious benefits; trust that your spirit is growing in intangible and mysterious ways.

**So far as a person gives,
he is free.**

The reward of a
gift well given is
to have given it.

**If you want to deny
yourself, deny others.**

To give and to receive is to feel the sun from both sides.

Not only is selfishness unrewarding, it's also exhausting.

Generosity always wins more respect than authority.

Give out
of the
door and
God will
put it
back
through
your
window.

Selflessness makes the self more significant.

When the blind man carries the lame man, both go forward.

No matter whether your life is long or short, its completeness rests upon what you gave.

Persist in giving and it becomes easier as your ability to give increases daily.

Be generous to everyone, young and old, weak and strong, because some day in your life you will have been all of these.

No individual has any right to come into the world and go out of it without leaving behind him distinct and legitimate reasons for having passed through it.

George Washington Carver

Generosity is like a radar that sees through the fog of inequality, poverty, and injustice.

You can choose to feel or express generosity; those that choose the second are the happiest.

For the truly generous, no miracles are necessary; they possess all the tools they need to change the world.

He who allows his day to pass by without practicing generosity and enjoying life's pleasures is like a blacksmith's bellows. He breathes, but does not live.

You need a lot of generosity to accomplish truly great things.

Are you a giver or a taker? If you are unsure, ask yourself this question: Do you eat well or sleep well?

In a perfect world, half of our happiness would arise from the generosity others show towards us, and the remainder would be the result of the generosity that we show to others.

Continuous generosity—not strength or intelligence—is the key to unlocking our capabilities.

If you give 100 per cent, God will make up the difference.

Generosity is concerned not with deciding whether something is good or bad but with how to make it work for others.

We take more out of
generosity than generosity
takes out of us.

**Life waxes or wanes
in proportion to
one's generosity.**

Happiness is ignoring those
who make generosity difficult.

If you strive to be generous instead of successful, you have already succeeded.

Your generosity can help others to shape their own destiny.

Only by restoring the severed connections in the world can we be healed.

Generous people are the ones who laugh all the way past the bank.

Generosity is like rowing upstream; not to advance is to drop back.

Successful people are always looking for opportunities to help others. Unsuccessful people are always asking, "What's in it for me?"

Brian Tracy

Getters don't get—
only givers get.

**If money got the world into this
mess, it can get us out of it too.**

A selfish person is like a bird who
spends its life walking because it
doesn't want to use its wings.

If you wish to excel at anything, excel at giving — the competition isn't that fierce.

Help your brother's boat across and your own will reach the shore.

Hindu proverb

Generosity is the key that unlocks the cabinet of God's treasures.

Generosity does not change the past, but it does make the future a better prospect.

Act like an angel and you may just end up becoming a saint.

Be generous, just for the fun of it!

What's the point of being selfish? It never helps anyone, least of all yourself.

If everyone showed a little more generosity there would be more happiness in the world than we would know what to do with.

It is easy to avoid giving, but you cannot avoid the consequences of avoiding.

I expect to pass through this world but once; any good thing therefore that I can do, or any kindness that I can show to any fellow creature, let me do it now; let me not defer or neglect it, for I shall not pass this way again.

Stephen Grellet

Joy is the overpowering secret of a benevolent soul.

Kindness is difficult to give away because it keeps coming back.

Become rich by spending time on others.

When you stop being generous, you give up your power to change.

If you want happiness, freedom, and peace of mind, the best way to get them is to give them to someone else.

Returning to give more than once is like rediscovering a secret.

The poorest is not the person without a cent, but without a gift.

Generosity forces us to perceive the world as it is meant to be.

Generosity brings us together because it allows us to experience the same things.

Make a promise that you won't allow yourself to go to bed each night unless you have performed a benevolent act during the day; you'll soon become a paragon of generosity even if it's just so you can get a little sleep.

What wisdom can you find that is greater than generosity?

Nothing but generosity has been able to save us from ourselves.

Generosity is the golden chain of good deeds that binds the world together.

Generosity makes ordinary people extraordinary.

Generosity is the feeling of smiling on the inside.

Where there is generosity there will be abundance even amid scarcity.

Generosity is the perfect solution to the puzzle of human existence.

The trouble with so many of us is that we underestimate the power of generosity and go searching for power everywhere else.

The novelty of sharing never wears off.

**Life without generosity
is like a tree without
blossoms or fruit.**

Everyone needs help
from everyone.
Bertolt Brecht

Generosity is a selfish act, if you call selfishness finding abundant peace and happiness for yourself.

Discover generosity and you reveal your own unique gifts.

Have you considered that the opposite of poverty isn't property—it's community.

He who is small in generosity will never be great in anything but failure.

If you bring sunshine into the lives of others, it will shine on you as well.

Chopping wood for others to burn warms you up too.

Give everything.
Want for nothing.

Generosity is a giant lever positioned on the fulcrum of this life, which enables us to move mountains in the next life.

For every minute you think of yourself, you lose 60 seconds of happiness.

The good deed you do today
For a brother or sister in need
Will come back to you some day
For humanity's a circle in deed.

Robert Alan

**Being generous means never
having to suffer the embarrassment
of hurrying past those in need
pretending they aren't there.**

If you are generous, every task is a noble one.

Generosity is the giving and so the receiving of life.

In everyone's life, at some time, our inner fire goes out. It is then burst into flame by an encounter with another human being. We should all be thankful for those people who rekindle the inner spirit.

Albert Schweitzer

The best way to surpass your own success is to share it.

A gift received becomes a blessing when you give it away.

Weave in generosity and God will find the thread.

Generosity is the unexpected spark that lights up the world.

Double the world's joy and halve its sorrow.

There is no great future for anyone whose generosity has dried up.

Those that flare up with generosity are destined to illuminate their time.

Be generous with your time and see how much more joy you cram into life.

Twenty years from now you will be more disappointed by the things that you kept than the things you gave away.

Give without cease and sleep in peace.

We make a living by what we get, but we make a life by what we give.

If you have anything really valuable to contribute to the world, it will come through the expression of your own personality, that single spark of divinity that sets you off and makes you different from every other living creature.

Bruce Barton

Count your blessings if others are counting on you.

You may have enthusiasm for ten minutes or for one month, but if you can keep it for 70 years you will lead a generous life.

The world is full of magical experiences waiting to happen after we begin to explore our generosity.

As a general rule,
the most guilty are
the least generous.

Thousands of candles can be
lit from a single candle, and
the life of the candle will not
be shortened.

If you give while you live, you'll get to see where it goes.

To give something up means setting it free. What can be more generous than that?

You have two choices when it comes to spreading light— to be the flame or the mirror that reflects it.

Edith Wharton

You are most likely to stumble upon happiness while attempting to make others happy.

The most solid comfort one can fall back upon is the thought that the business of one's life is to help in some small way to reduce the sum of ignorance, degradation, and misery on the face of this beautiful earth.

George Eliot

Don't give until it hurts; give until it feels good.

Overcome the fear and distrust of others with faith and generosity.

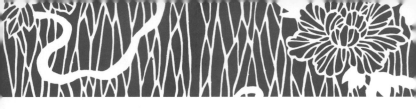

If you see anybody fallen by the wayside and lying in the ditch, it isn't much good climbing into the ditch and lying by his side.

H. R. L. Sheppard

If you give me a fish, it will feed me for a day. If you teach me how to fish, it will feed me for the rest of my life.

We are living in a time of great abundance, perhaps the greatest ever. Why do we act like it is a time of scarcity? Are we ruled by fear rather than love?

Ken Neher

When generosity and skill work together, expect miracles.

A spark of generosity starts a fire of love.

You may be disappointed if you don't accept but you are doomed if you don't give.

If you have more than you need, it tends to hold you back from the business of being.

If Rosa Parks had not refused to move to the back of the bus, you and I might never have heard of Dr. Martin Luther King.

Ramsey Clark

Out of compassion I destroy
the darkness of their ignorance.
From within them I light the
lamp of wisdom and dispel all
darkness from their lives.

Bhagavad Gita

**If you can develop a keen
awareness of the interdependence
of all living things you will soon
understand why generosity helps
all humanity.**

One more good person on earth is better than an extra angel in heaven.

Generosity
is contagious.
Start an
epidemic today.

Published by MQ Publications Limited
12 The Ivories, 6–8 Northampton Street
London N1 2HY
email: mqpublications.com
website: www.mqpublications.com

Editor: Karen Ball
Design concept: Broadbase
Design: Philippa Jarvis

ISBN: 1-84072-562-1

10 9 8 7 6 5 4 3 2

Printed and bound in China